YOUNG DISCOVERERS

RIVERS AND OCEANS

BARBARA TAYLOR

KING*f*ISHER

KINGFISHER
Kingfisher Publications Plc
New Penderel House
283–288 High Holborn
London WC1V 7HZ
www.kingfisherpub.com

First published by Kingfisher
Publications Plc 1992
This edition published 2001
10 9 8 7 6 5 4 3 2

2TR / 0401 / WKT / HBM (UNV) / 128KMA

A CIP catalogue record for this book is
available from the British Library.

ISBN 0 86272 978 5

Series editor: Sue Nicholson
Series design: Terry Woodley
Cover design: Pinpoint Design Company
Design: Ben White
Picture research: Elaine Willis
Illustrations: Hayward Art Group pp.4 (top),
    5 (top), 6 (bottom), 8 (left), 9 (top), 12 (top
    right and bottom left), 14 (left), 22-23, 24
    (bottom right), 25 (top); Kevin Maddison
    pp.4-5 (bottom), 6 (top), 8 (bottom), 10-11,
    12 (bottom), 14-21, 23 (bottom right), 24
    (top), 25 (bottom), 26 (bottom), 28, 29
    (left), 30 (bottom left), 31 (right); Janos
    Marffy, Kathy Jakeman Illustration pp.7, 8
    (top right), 9 (bottom), 11 (top), 13, 15 (top
    right), 18 (right), 23 (top), 24 (bottom left),
    27, 30, 31; Simon Tegg, Simon Girling &
    Associates pp.26 (top), 29 (right)
Photographs: Harold Berger p.10, Alan Cork
    p.19, Dennis Gilbert p.29, Hutchison
    Library pp.15, 16, 20; ZEFA p.13

Phototypeset by Southern Positives and
Negatives (SPAN), Lingfield, Surrey

Printed in Hong Kong / China
2(1BP)/0799/WKT/HBM(UNV)/128KMA

About This Book

This book tells you about rivers, lakes and oceans and how they shape the land. It also gives you lots of ideas for projects and things to look out for. You should be able to find nearly everything you need to do the projects around your home. You may need to buy some items, but they are all cheap and easy to find. Be careful when you are studying a river out of doors. Do not go near rivers, lakes or any open water on your own – always go with an adult.

Activity Hints

- Before you begin, read the instructions carefully and collect all the things you need.
- When you have finished, clear everything away, especially sharp things like knives and scissors, and wash your hands.

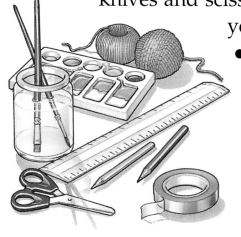

- Start a special notebook. Keep a record of what you do in each project and the things that you find out.

Contents

Water in our World

Almost three-quarters of the Earth's surface is covered with water, making the planet look blue from Space. Water is essential to life on Earth. Without it, all animals and plants would die. Oceans and seas make up most of the world's water. But there is also water in the sky, in the form of clouds. Rain or snow falls from the clouds and collects in lakes, rivers and glaciers (rivers of ice). Water and ice have the power to change the shape of the land.

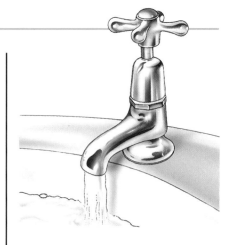

How much water do you use a day? In Western Europe, North America and some parts of Asia, every person uses over two bathtubs full!

👁 Eye-Spy

Do you live near a stream or a river, or even by the sea? Why not start a scrapbook about it. Paste in photographs or drawings to show its wildlife and how people use the water.

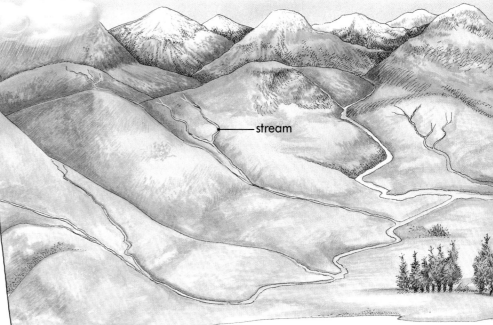

stream

Many rivers start in hills and mountains as small, fast-flowing streams. As the water rushes downhill, it cuts deep valleys through the land.

In the middle part of a river, the water flows more slowly in a wide, flat valley. The river curves from side to side in loops called meanders.

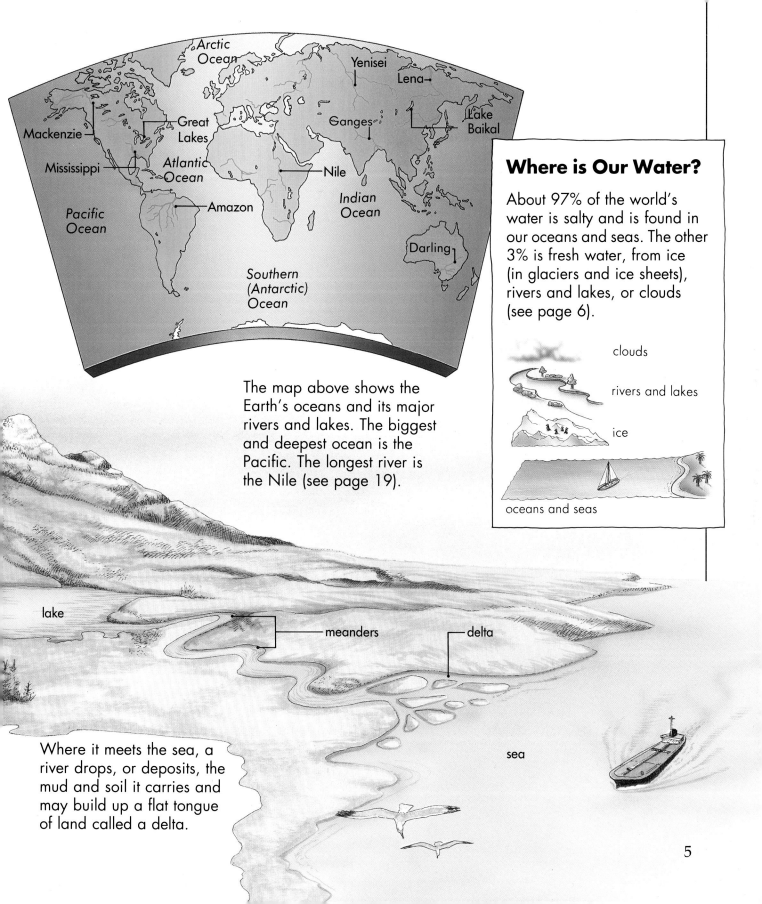

Arctic
Ocean

Yenisei

Lena→

Mackenzie

Great
Lakes

Ganges

Lake
Baikal

Mississippi

Atlantic
Ocean

Nile

Pacific
Ocean

Amazon

Indian
Ocean

Darling

Southern
(Antarctic)
Ocean

The map above shows the
Earth's oceans and its major
rivers and lakes. The biggest
and deepest ocean is the
Pacific. The longest river is
the Nile (see page 19).

Where is Our Water?

About 97% of the world's
water is salty and is found in
our oceans and seas. The other
3% is fresh water, from ice
(in glaciers and ice sheets),
rivers and lakes, or clouds
(see page 6).

clouds

rivers and lakes

ice

oceans and seas

lake

meanders

delta

sea

Where it meets the sea, a
river drops, or deposits, the
mud and soil it carries and
may build up a flat tongue
of land called a delta.

The Water Cycle

Did you know that the total amount of water on Earth is the same as it was over 4000 million years ago? This is because water rains down from the sky then rises up again in a never-ending journey called the water cycle. The Sun heats the liquid water in rivers, lakes and oceans, turning some of it into an invisible gas called water vapour. The water vapour evaporates, or disappears into the air. If the air rises and cools down, the water vapour condenses, or turns back into droplets of liquid water.

Mark the edge of a puddle with chalk, string or a row of pebbles and time how long it takes for the water to evaporate. Do puddles dry up faster in the sunshine or in the shade?

Water All Around

Water falls from clouds as rain or snow (1) and collects in rivers, lakes, seas and oceans (2). The Sun's heat turns some water into water vapour in the air (3). The air rises and cools and some water vapour turns back into liquid water, forming clouds (4).

Do it yourself

Plants take up water through their roots and give off water through their leaves. If you grow plants in a sealed jar, they will be able to use the same water over and over again, just like the Earth's real water cycle.

3. Put the top on the bottle and leave it in a shady place.

4. See how water given off by the plants condenses on the cool sides of the bottle and runs down into the soil. The plants can use the water again and again.

More Things to Try

Ask an adult to hold a spoon in the jet of steam from a boiling kettle. Watch how water condenses on the cold spoon to form droplets – just like the raindrops falling from clouds.

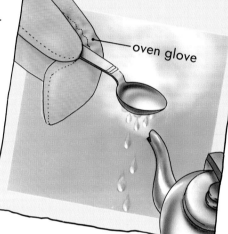

oven glove

spoon tied to the end of a stick

drops of water

1. Place a large plastic bottle on its side and spoon in a layer of gravel with a layer of soil or special potting compost on top.

2. Use thin sticks to push small plants, such as ivy, ferns and mosses, into the soil. Press down the soil around the plants with a cotton reel tied to a stick.

Water Under the Ground

Some of the water that falls as rain soaks into the ground, slowly trickling down through tiny air spaces in soil or through cracks in rocks. Eventually, the water reaches a layer of rock – called impermeable rock – that will not allow water to pass through it. The rocks just above this impermeable rock layer become soaked with water, forming pockets or reservoirs of water called aquifers. The highest level of water in an aquifer is called the water table.

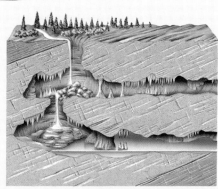

Water easily wears away soft rocks like limestone, forming tunnels and caves. As water drips through cave roofs, it evaporates, leaving behind rocky pillars called stalactites and stalagmites.

stalactite

stalagmite

Desert Oases

In a desert, it hardly ever rains. However, moist areas called oases are found in places where water-filled rocks are near the Earth's surface. The water may have soaked into mountains hundreds of kilometres away, draining down through the rocks under the desert.

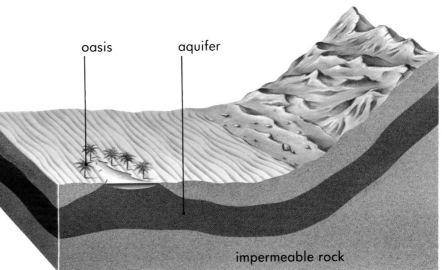

oasis

aquifer

impermeable rock

Do it yourself

Try making your own stalactites and stalagmites. You need two jars, a saucer, wool, washing soda and water.

1. Fill the jars with warm water and stir in plenty of washing soda, making sure that all the soda dissolves, or disappears, in the water.

2. Stand the jars in a warm, safe place with the saucer between them.

3. Loop a piece of wool from one jar to the other so that each end can soak up the water.

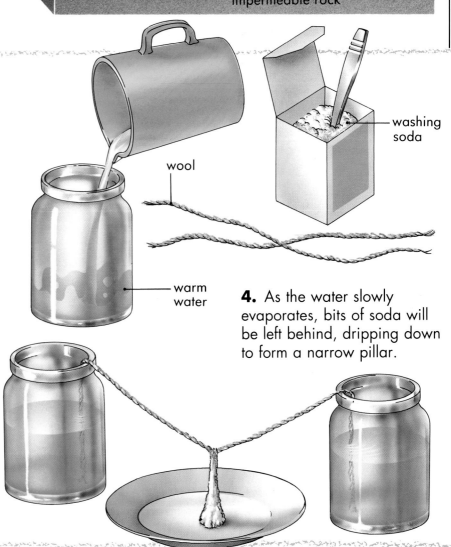

washing soda

wool

warm water

4. As the water slowly evaporates, bits of soda will be left behind, dripping down to form a narrow pillar.

9

Rivers of Ice

In areas where there is snow all year round, water may be frozen into huge ice sheets or 'rivers of ice', called glaciers. Glaciers can be up to 400 kilometres long and are often 300 metres thick. They form when piles of snow are squashed together to make ice – in the same way that a snowball goes hard when you press the snow together. The ice in a glacier becomes so thick and heavy that it slides slowly downhill.

The bottom end of a glacier is called its snout. Here it is warmer, so the ice melts to form streams of icy water called meltwater.

Glaciers start high up in mountains or near the North and South Poles where it is very cold. Snow piles up in layers and is squashed and frozen into ice.

As the glacier moves slowly downhill, it grinds and scrapes the land beneath, carrying away rocks and boulders and gouging out a deep, wide valley.

The ice on the surface of a glacier is brittle, like toffee. As the glacier moves, the ice can snap, forming jagged pinnacles and deep cracks called crevasses.

Do it yourself

See how the pieces of rock carried by a glacier scrape against the land beneath, creating a force called friction which slows the glacier down.

Make two blocks of ice as shown on the right. Which 'glacier' moves more slowly when you slide it down the slope?

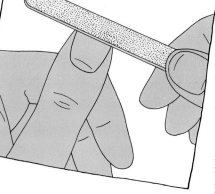

water

gravel and water

Eye-Spy

The pieces of rock carried by a glacier make its sides and bottom rough. Glaciers smooth and polish the rocks they move over in the same way that a rough nail file smooths a broken fingernail.

After the Ice

After glaciers have melted, we can find clues that tell us where they used to be. These include hollows with steep walls (called cirques) and deep U-shaped valleys.

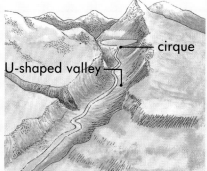

cirque

U-shaped valley

snout

River Sources

The source or beginning of most rivers is rainwater which collects in small hollows or gullies and trickles over the surface of the land. This water does not soak into the soil or the rocks below because the rocks are either already full of water or will not let water pass through them. The trickles of water join up into a stream and several streams flow together to make a river. Other rivers start as mountain springs (see the box on the right) or flow from lakes, marshes or glaciers.

Mountain Springs

Rainwater may collect under the ground, above impermeable rock layers through which it cannot pass. Where these rock layers reach the surface, the water above gushes out as a mountain spring.

Many rivers begin in natural hollows, which fill up with water to form ponds or lakes.

Source of the Nile

The world's longest river is the Nile. Its main source is Lake Victoria in Uganda, Africa. The river flows north through Sudan and Egypt to the Mediterranean Sea. See page 19 for more about the River Nile.

Rivers at Work

Streams and rivers have the power to change the shape of the land. But water on its own is not strong enough to wear land away. It is all the boulders, pebbles and grains of sand carried along by the water that give a river its cutting force. Sometimes, however, swirling water may split rocks apart by forcing air into cracks in the rock. Some rocks may also be eaten away by chemicals carried in water.

Over millions of years, the Colorado River in Arizona, the United States, has carved out a huge channel called the Grand Canyon.

Do it yourself

Make your own river and see how it carves out a path downhill.

1. Outside, build a sloping mountain out of damp sand, pebbles and mud.

2. Slowly pour a steady stream of water over the top of the mountain. Watch carefully to see how the water finds the quickest way down the slope and how much sand and gravel it carries.

damp sand and gravel

Rushing Rivers

At the start of its course, a river flows quickly, ripping up loose stones and pebbles and hurling them at the sides and bed of the river. After a storm, a river often contains more water, so it is able to pick up and carry huge boulders. With this material, called its load, the river pounds away at the land, cutting downwards to form a steep-sided valley shaped like the letter V. This part of a river's course often has waterfalls and rapids – stretches of very fast-flowing water.

A Waterfall is Born

Different kinds of rock wear away at different speeds. So where water flows over bands of soft rock and hard rock (1), the soft rock is worn away first, leaving a step of hard rock (2). Over thousands of years, more soft rock is worn away and the step becomes steeper (3). The water tumbles over the step as a waterfall.

Waterfalls may also form when rivers plunge over the sides of steep valleys that have been gouged out by glaciers, or over cliffs pushed up by the movement of the Earth.

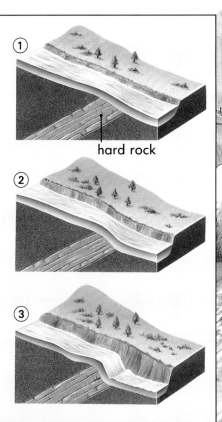

hard rock

14

The drawing below shows the round dips or holes that you can often see in a dry river bed. These pot-holes are formed when water swirls pebbles round and round, wearing out hollows. The water swirls faster as the hollows get deeper.

pot-hole

👁 Eye-Spy

Put some gravel in a clear plastic container then hold it under fast-flowing water to see how the water swirls the gravel around.

Right: Waterfalls on the River Iguacu, on the borders of Brazil and Argentina in South America.

Winding Rivers

Where the land is less steep, the river begins to flow more slowly, cutting sideways into the land rather than downwards. The river now contains more water because other rivers and streams – called tributaries – have joined it, and it carries a greater load. The slower-moving water does not have enough power to carry all its load away, so some of the material drops to the river bed and settles there.

When a river flows slowly, the water takes the easy route around small humps or hillocks rather than rushing over them. This makes the river swing or meander from side to side.

This meandering river looks brown and muddy because of all the sand and soil that it is carrying. A river drops more and more of its load as it slows down.

levee

meander

Do it yourself

Work out the speed of a river's current and watch how water flows faster on the outside of a curve.

Push two marker sticks into the river bank, about 100 metres apart. Drop a twig into the water by one marker and time how long it takes to reach the other marker.

Watch how your twigs flow around curves. Where do they flow the fastest?

The wide, flat valley floor is called a floodplain. During a flood, the river may break through its banks, leaving behind gravel, sand and mud, which build up in high banks called levees.

After a lot of rain, when there is more water in a river, the river may cut through the 'neck' of a meander. This leaves behind a banana-shaped lake called an ox-bow lake.

ox-bow lake   floodplain

Floods in China

The Huang He in China has flooded over 1500 times since people began living there. In 1887, the flood was so bad that over one million people died.

Winding Rivers

The point where a river meets the sea is called the river's mouth. Here, the river slows down even further, dropping more and more of its load. Deltas often form at river mouths when the material dropped by the river builds up a fan-shaped area of flat, marshy land. The river splits into smaller channels, flowing around islands of new land to the sea.

 Eye-Spy

Deltas got their name because most of them are triangular in shape, like the Greek letter 'delta'.

Do it yourself

Do this experiment to see how a river's load sinks faster in salty water than it does in fresh water.

Put the same amount of soil and water in two clear plastic containers but add two or three teaspoonfuls of salt to one of them. Watch how the grains of mud in the salty water stick together and sink to the bottom.

salty water

fresh water

The new land made around a delta is almost flat. So when there is a lot of rain, rivers on deltas often break out of their channels and flood the land. Every year, many people living on the Ganges-Brahmaputra Delta in Bangladesh are injured or even killed by heavy floods.

The Nile

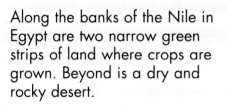

The world's longest river, the Nile, is actually made up of two rivers – the White Nile and the Blue Nile. Near the source of the river, at Lake Victoria, there are many rapids and waterfalls. Where the river joins the sea, 6695 kilometres away, there is a vast delta. In August and September, the Nile floods because of heavy rains near its source. The floodwaters used to spread rich soil over the farmers' fields in Egypt, but they are now held back behind the Aswan High Dam.

Famers rely on the waters of the Nile to keep their crops alive. They use machines like this Archimedes screw to raise water from the river up to their fields.

Along the banks of the Nile in Egypt are two narrow green strips of land where crops are grown. Beyond is a dry and rocky desert.

Aswan High Dam

The Aswan High Dam was built to control floods, provide a regular water supply and help to make electricity.

19

Lakes

Lakes are large hollows filled with rainwater, or the water from rivers or streams. They may be formed when glaciers, rivers, the wind, or movements deep inside the Earth create dips or channels in the land. Some lakes are made when water is held back by a barrier, such as the rocks left by glaciers or the hardened rock that once gushed out of volcanoes as liquid lava.

Although some of the world's lakes are huge, no lake lasts forever. They all eventually evaporate, fill with soil and plants or are drained by rivers.

Beavers may create a lake by building a dam of sticks and mud across a river. They then build their home, called a lodge, in the middle of the new lake, where it is safe.

Left: The Dead Sea, in the Middle East, is really a lake. Rivers flowing into the Dead Sea carry so much salt from rocks high in the mountains that the lake's water is eight times saltier than sea water. People are able to float easily in such salty water.

Below: On the floor of the Great Rift Valley in East Africa is a chain of long, narrow and deep lakes, including Lake Victoria, Lake Malawi, Lake Tanganyika and Lake Nakuru. Lake Nakuru is famous for its thousands of beautiful pink flamingos.

Loch Ness Monster?

Some people believe that the relatives of a huge pre-historic monster live in the deep waters of the Scottish lake, Loch Ness. But no-one has been able to prove this by taking a clear photograph.

Six Deepest Lakes

Lake Baikal in northern Asia is the world's deepest and oldest lake. It also contains the most water.

Baikal (1620 m)
Tanganyika (1435 m)
Caspian Sea (995 m)
Malawi/Nyasa (700 m)
Great Bear Lake (411 m)
Superior (406 m)

Oceans and Seas

Most of the world's water is contained in its five oceans – the Arctic, Atlantic, Indian, Pacific and Southern (or Antarctic). Most of the Arctic Ocean is frozen and covered with ice. During the summer some of the ice melts, releasing huge blocks of drifting ice called pack ice, or smaller chunks called icebergs.

The world's seas are much smaller than the oceans. The seas are usually close to, or surrounded by, the Earth's land.

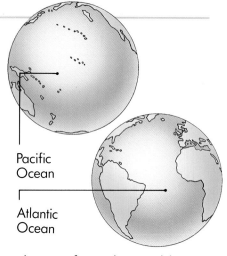

Pacific Ocean

Atlantic Ocean

The Pacific is the world's largest ocean – it is bigger than all the Earth's land put together.

Exploring the Deep

The land at the bottom of the oceans is not flat. It has huge mountains, deep valleys and even volcanoes. Scientists use submersibles, like this one, to explore the ocean depths.

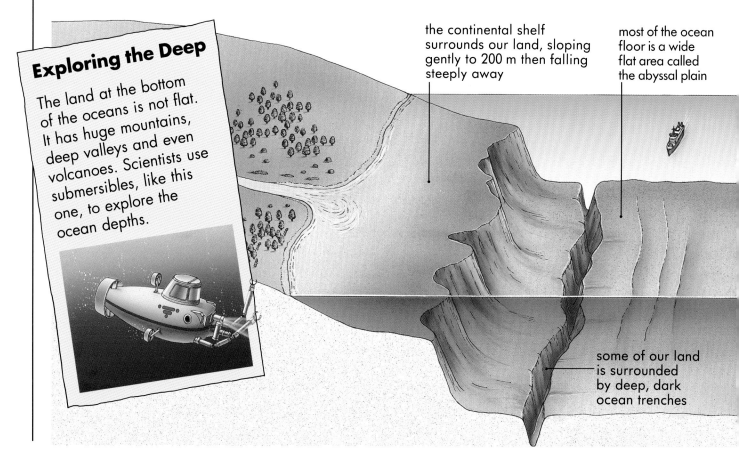

the continental shelf surrounds our land, sloping gently to 200 m then falling steeply away

most of the ocean floor is a wide flat area called the abyssal plain

some of our land is surrounded by deep, dark ocean trenches

Do it yourself

Make your own floating iceberg. All you need is a balloon, a bucket or a bowl – and some water!

Follow the stages shown in the drawings. (Ask an adult to help you stretch the neck of the balloon over a cold tap and knot the end when it is full of water.) See how much of your iceberg floats below the water's surface.

fill the balloon with water

cut the balloon away with scissors after the water has been frozen

the hidden part of an iceberg can be dangerous to ships

mountain ranges called mid-oceanic ridges run along parts of the ocean floor

some mountains break the ocean's surface to form island chains

Deep Sea Fishes

The Sun's light and heat cannot reach deep down in the oceans, so it is dark and cold there. Many deep sea fishes, like this angler fish, produce their own light to help them find food.

Waves, Currents and Tides

The water in our seas and oceans is always moving, even when it looks calm and still. Winds blowing across the water make ripples, or waves, on the sea's surface, and create sweeping ocean currents. The level of the sea also rises and falls every day in a regular pattern of high and low tides. Tides are caused mainly by the pull of the Moon as it circles the Earth. Sometimes, huge waves called tsunamis are set off by underwater earthquakes and volcanoes.

A wave's size depends on the speed of the wind, and how long and how far the wind has been blowing.

Eye-Spy

Have you ever made waves in the bath? To see how waves work, watch a bath toy, like a duck, bob up and down on a wave rather than moving forwards.

How Waves Work

In the open sea, waves look like they are travelling forwards, but the water in each wave stays in almost the same place, moving round in circles. Near the shore, some of the water catches on the seabed. This slows the wave down and the top of the wave curves over and breaks.

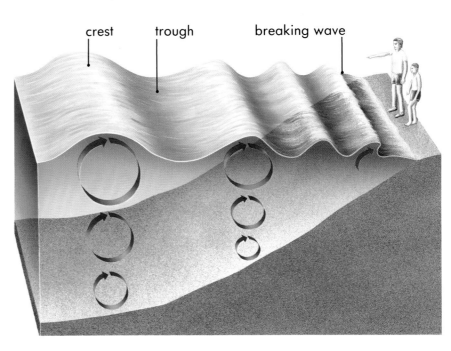

crest   trough   breaking wave

Ocean Currents

Ocean currents are like giant rivers, flowing slowly across the oceans and seas. There are nearly 40 main currents in the world's oceans. Warm currents, shown on this map in red, flow near the water's surface. They are created by winds. Cold currents, shown in green, are created when cold water sinks and spreads. They move deep down in the ocean depths.

At high tide, the sea rises up the shore, dumping seaweed, shells, feathers, wood and other objects in a ragged line called the strandline.

Most coasts have two high tides and two low tides every 24 hours.

Waves at Work

Waves carry with them the energy and power of the wind. Strong waves hurl rocks and pebbles against the coasts, wearing away cliffs. Breaking waves pound against rocks, squashing air into rock cracks. Then, when the waves pull back, the squashed air explodes out, weakening the rock and eventually breaking it apart. Cliff bases become worn away by the pounding waves until the upper parts overhang. This weakens the cliffs until large sections of rock may crumble into the sea.

Soft rocks, like chalk or limestone, wear away quickly. Houses built on soft cliffs may fall into the sea as the rocks beneath are cut away.

Shaping the Coast

Soft rock is worn away to make bays, while hard rock juts out as headlands. Waves may punch a hole called a blowhole through the roof of a cave. Or caves on opposite sides of a headland may meet to form an arch. If the roof of an arch falls in, it leaves a column of rock called a stack.

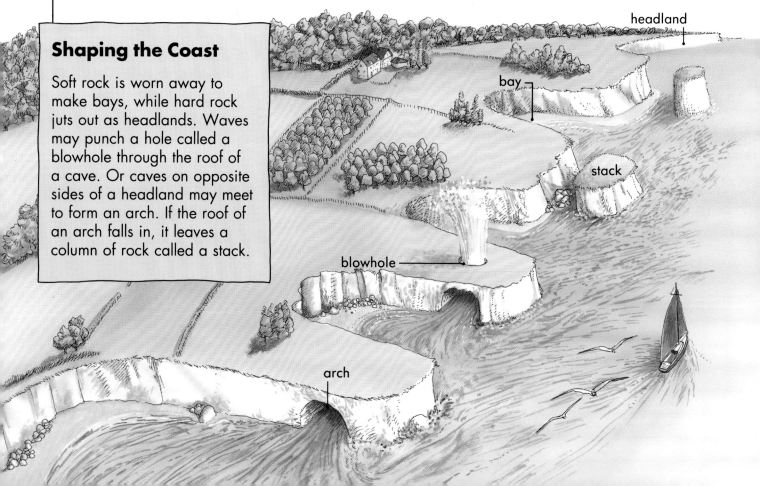

Do it yourself

See how many different pebbles you can find if you visit the seashore. You may even spot pieces of semi-precious stones, such as jet, agate and jasper.

Look for pebbles that are different colours, shapes and sizes. See if you can find any with holes right through. Some pebbles have coloured bands of different rocks running through them. Others sparkle in the light.

👁 Eye-Spy

As you suck a sweet, it becomes smoother and rounder. In the same way, the rough edges of rocks become smooth as they roll around in the sea.

More Things to Try

To make a pebble picture, draw a simple shape on a piece of thick card. Sort out groups of small pebbles of the same size and colour, glue them down and varnish them.

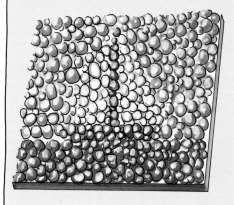

There are many ways of sorting out your pebble collection. If you keep them in a clear container filled with water, the colours will show up well.

Waves at Work

Sand, pebbles and grains of rock and soil are washed onto our coasts by waves or dropped into the sea at river mouths. In sheltered areas, this material builds up to form beaches. On some beaches, the wind blows sand into small hills, or dunes. On headlands, sand may build up into a narrow ridge called a spit. The wind and waves can easily blow or wash away fine sand. To stop our coasts wearing away, people plant grasses, like marram grasses, or build fences, called groynes.

Marram grass grows quickly on sand dunes. Its roots bind the sand together and stop it from drifting away.

Building a Spit

Where a coasts curves, waves may carry sand and pebbles on in a straight line, building a long ridge, or a spit.

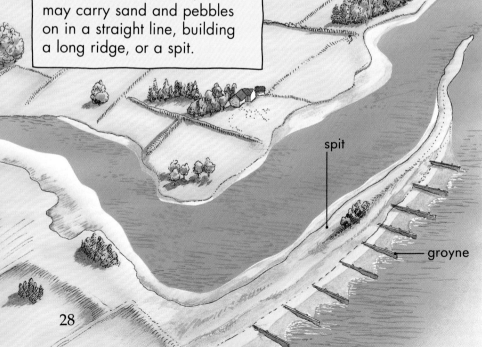

spit

groyne

Longshore Drift

If waves hit a beach at an angle, they move the sand along in a zig-zag path called longshore drift.

28

Water Pollution

The Earth's water is much more polluted, or dirtier, than it used to be. Sewage, chemicals used on crops and waste from factories are washed into rivers, lakes and the oceans. And leaks and spills from oil tankers add to this pollution. Fishes and other creatures find it difficult to survive in polluted waters and this upsets the balance of life on Earth.

Pollution of the air, or atmosphere, may be heating the whole world. This could make the ice sheets at the Poles melt, causing sea levels to rise and sea water to flood the land.

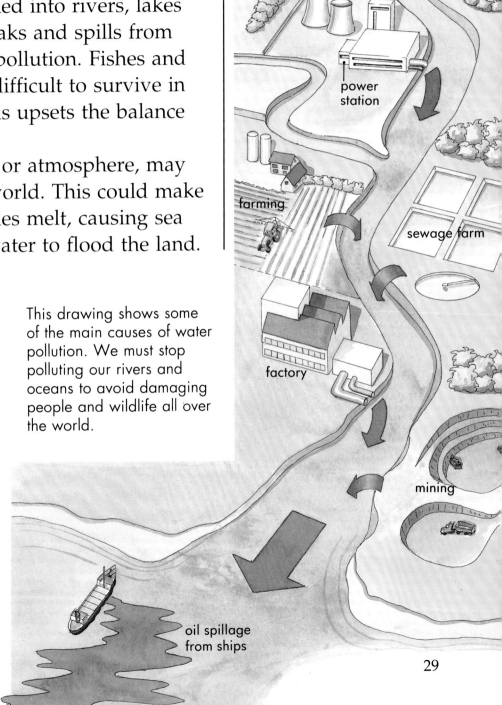

refuse site

power station

farming

sewage farm

factory

mining

oil spillage from ships

Oil Damage

Oil sticks birds' feathers together so they cannot fly or swim – the birds will die unless their feathers can be cleaned.

This drawing shows some of the main causes of water pollution. We must stop polluting our rivers and oceans to avoid damaging people and wildlife all over the world.

29

Do it yourself

Make a water filter to clean up some dirty water.

1. Make some muddy water by mixing soil, sand, leaves and twigs in an old container and pouring the mixture through a sieve.

2. Cut the bottom off a large plastic bottle and wedge some cotton wool in its neck.

3. Turn the bottle upside down and support it in a jar. Add a layer of gravel and sand over the cotton wool, then a sheet of blotting paper. These layers trap the dirt.

4. Pour the muddy water through the filter – but do not drink it. The filtered water is still very dirty!

soil, sand, leaves and twigs

👁 Eye-Spy

Make a record of any water pollution near your home. Look out for rubbish and litter by river banks or shores and for oil or factory wastes floating on the water.

scum on side of bottle

blotting paper

muddy water

sand

gravel

cotton wool

glass to collect water

filtered water

Amazing Rivers and Oceans

Although we know much more about the power of our rivers and oceans than people living long ago, the world under the sea is still a mysterious and dangerous place.

Do it yourself

Why not start a fact file about rivers and oceans?

Divide your file into sections and use a ring-binder so that you can add new pages to each section as you discover and learn more.

Collect postcards, stamps and photographs and cut out pictures from magazines.

Scientists are still making exciting discoveries about the world under the sea, so look out for newspaper articles about new developments or undersea expeditions.

Record Breakers

- Largest ocean – Pacific (181,000,000 sq km)
- Smallest ocean – Arctic (12,257,000 sq km)
- Deepest point on Earth – Mariana Trench, Pacific Ocean (11,033 m deep)
- Highest waterfall – Angel Falls, South America (979 m)
- Longest river – Nile (6695 m)
- Largest saltwater lake – Caspian Sea (371,800 sq km)
- Largest freshwater lake – Lake Superior, North America (82,350 sq km)
- Deepest lake – Lake Baikal, northern Asia (1620 m)
- Highest sea wave ever recorded (34 m high)
- Longest glacier – Lambert-Fisher Ice Passage, Antarctica (400 km long)
- Largest delta – Ganges-Brahmaputra (75,000 sq km)

Index